# THROUGH OUR EYES

*To Rita
from Rose*

The 20th Century
as seen by the

## San Francisco Chronicle

**San Francisco Chronicle**

Richard T. Thieriot
*Editor and Publisher*

**"Through Our Eyes" Staff**

Howard I. Finberg
*Editor and designer*

Gary Fong & Bryan Moss
*Assistant picture editors*

John P. Sullivan
*Cover design and typography*

Charles Denson & Jim Parkinson
*Assistant artists*

Pamela Reasner
*Captions*

Bill Van Niekerken
*Research*

Steve Ringman
*Section page photographs*

David Ballard
*Editorial assistant*

*Cameras courtesy of
Charlie Denson,
Art Frisch and
the Joe Dee Museum of Photography*

Chronicle Publishing Company
901 Mission Street
San Francisco, Ca. 94119

Distributed to the book trade by
Chronicle Books
1 Hallidie Plaza
San Francisco, CA 94102

Library of Congress cataloging and publication data available
Printed in the United States of America

ISBN 87701-467-1

As an old print merchant, I used to resent the aphorism, "A picture is worth a thousand words," until somebody observed, "It took words to say that." My tender ego was further assuaged when a press agent was quoted as saying, "A word in Caen's column is worth a thousand pictures," a proposition I am not prepared to defend or even discuss.

That personal hurdle cleared, let us discuss the subject at hand. Pictures. Not just pictures — photographs. Not just photographs but press photographs, most of them taken in the white heat of deadline pressure, all of them produced by one of the most celebrated teams in the history of American journalism, the photographers of the San Francisco Chronicle.

If The Chronicle's prose has sometimes been shaky — especially that appearing for the past 50-odd years under a certain byline — the art, imagination and timeliness of the paper's photographers have been and continue to be of the highest quality. A complete list of the awards they have won would fill this page. Of even more importance are the jealous accolades of peers who mutter, "Gawd, you guys have a crazy bunch of photoggers!" Crazier than coots, more fearless than daredevils and dedicated as only true professionals can be, they are The Chronicle's glory, their work captured in glorious black and white for all time, provided somebody didn't misplace the damn negative.

The public perception of a press photographer probably is lower than that of those who have the privilege of working with them. Most people see them as pushy and tough, badgering and even shouting at a beleaguered president, sticking their nosy lenses into private sorrow, getting in the way at public events, talking a beauty queen into lifting her dress just a little higher, looking for the most unflattering angle of a public personage they detest. The cliche was best or worst personified by the photographer in the TV newspaper series, "Lou Grant." His nickname was "Animal" and he lived down to it in appearance, all the while being a fine person deep down inside.

In what we imagine to be real life, they come in all sizes and shapes, their manner ranging from poetic introspection to salty wisecracking. All of them seem to have the same God-given quality of spotting the shot almost immediately, their instincts zeroing in on the angle we would never think of. Their minds must be like super-fast shutters, recording a series of scenes before the camera is even out of its case. They can "see" the shot cropped and printed (sometimes lamentably badly with rare exceptions — reproduction on newsprint is no match for the crisp clarity of the original print, a fact that drives the more sensitive photographers wild as an — OK — "Animal").

I don't go back quite far enough to remember powder flash, which sometimes singed the eyebrows off photographer and subject alike, but I do remember the long years of the Speed Graphic, the dominant camera of the pre-compact era. It was heavy, bulky, difficult to focus and carried a flash attachment big enough to light up the Golden Gate Bridge; yet, the old-timers got splendid results with it. It was the Speed Graphic that established the image of the press photographer, hat perched on the back of his head, boxy camera at his eye, explosive flash bulb highlighting expressions of joy, dismay, distress.

The Chronicle had a colorful crew in the Speed Graphic era. The most celebrated — in legend, at least — was "Borny" Bjornmuller, who aimed his flash bulb at Queen Marie of Romania and barked, "If you want your pitcha in The Chronicle, look over here, Queen!" (the foregoing is only one version of whatever Borny actually said, but the idea is the same). There was the supreme sourpuss, Clem Albers, who looked totally bored by the entire process but always came back with a superb and original picture. There was Barney Peterson, who looked like a Marine and became one during World War II, who barked at subjects like a drill sergeant and made them like it as they quavered, "You want me to do WHAT?" There was and is Bill Young, a rough-talking, good-hearted bear who, for unfathomable reasons, caught the fancy of San Francisco's notoriously ingrown social crowd; at all the best parties, he was in demand by the beauties who said, "And don't forget an extra copy for me, Bill, dear." And there was and is Joe Rosenthal, whose shot of the Iwo Jima flag-raising put him on the all-time list, this smallish, mild-mannered, sweet-smiling guy in a beret. His fame is not his fortune; everybody but Joe made a bundle off his immortal photo.

As this brilliant collection attests, The Chronicle's current crew of photographers, liberated from the elephantine Speed Graphic, more than lives up to the heady standards of the trailblazers. There are classics in this book, classics of humor and pathos, timeless tributes to the split-second imagination of the person behind the viewfinder, the inevitable instances of blind luck that reward the sharpest of eyes. It would be a disservice to single out any one photograph. They are all the exciting result of art under intense pressure.

In this age of high technology, I am still most impressed by the daily production of a large and complicated newspaper. The task is herculean and the deadlines impossible, but somehow the product emerges, more or less on time. And if the result is above the norm, the credit generally goes to "Hey, one great shot!," the priceless contribution of those whose work is memorialized here.

News photography has played an important part in the tradition of journalism in the San Francisco Bay Area. The Chronicle has always had talented photographers on its staff. "Through Our Eyes" tries to portray both the changing nature of events covered by the newspaper since the turn of the century and the changing style and importance of newspaper photography during the same period.

Each decade has its own style, as both equipment and photographers change; each is reflective of the advances in technique and technology.

To compile and edit the pictures for this book, Gary Fong, Bryan Moss and I spent weeks looking through folders of photographs and drawers of negatives. Sometimes we were surprised by what we found, other times disappointed. Many photographers in the early part of this century did not view their work as having lasting value and were not as careful in filing and preserving their prints and negatives as today's photographers. This accounts for the lack of attribution on many of the older pictures in this book.

Today's photographers face the same challenges as the men and women who worked before them. They sometimes cover the dangerous, exciting story, but more likely are trying to capture a strong image for a story not yet written about a topic not easily explained. This is a challenge faced by every photographer at every newspaper in every country.

When the photographer returns to the office, picture editors begin to apply rules as they sort through negatives and prints. First, the photograph must have strong news or feature value as defined by that day's events and the amount of space available in the paper. Second, the picture must at least meet the minimum requirements as a piece of photographic work. But to compile the photographs for this book a third standard needed to be applied: The photograph must have lasting value as either an interesting example of the prevailing style of news photography or as a representation of people and events that were significant to the newspaper's readers. To select photographs that meet these tests is a difficult job.

Fortunately, the process could begin on a solid foundation. Ten years ago, The Chronicle published a 128-page catalog in connection with an exhibition of photographs at the San Francisco Museum of Modern Art. The exhibition, called "...a thousand words," was the idea of Gordon Peters, the paper's chief photographer, now retired, and had the strong support of the paper's publisher, Richard T. Thieriot. Using the catalog as a starting point, photographs were added and deleted for this book.

The purpose of "Through Our Eyes" is not necessarily to record history but rather to present a "snapshot" of news photography as practiced by Chronicle photographers, past and present. We also hope to delight and surprise you with pictures that have lasting impact, pictures that offer glimpses of people and events seen by journalists working with cameras and film rather than pencil and paper.

Howard I. Finberg
*Photography and Graphics Editor*
**San Francisco Chronicle**

*April 1987*

# THE
# EARLY
# YEARS

GRAFLEX

**THE EARLY YEARS**

*From top left:* Earthquake survivors camping out in Golden Gate Park;
the ruined city; refugees at lunch; a looter is executed. *1906*.

## THE EARLY YEARS

A United Railroads streetcar along Fillmore Street. *1907.*

## THE EARLY YEARS

*Top:* A busy day at Ocean Beach. *1907.*

Bathers at Ocean Beach below the original Cliff House. *1907.*

**THE EARLY YEARS**

Lincoln Beachey flying in front of the Palace of Fine Arts, Pan Pacific Exposition. *1915*.

## THE EARLY YEARS

*Top:* Pilot Silas Christofferson, who made the first S. F.-L. A. flight in February. *1914*.

The first plane to take off from a ship leaving the cruiser Pennsylvania in the bay. *1911*.

## THE EARLY YEARS

Troops marching down Market Street in a homecoming parade at the end of World War I. *1918*.

The Graf Zeppelin flying over San Francisco on its trip from Tokyo to Los Angeles. *1929*.

# THE 30s

SPEED GRAPHIC

After battering down the San Jose jail door, a mob hangs Thomas Thurmond, alleged kidnaper-killer of Brooke Hart, 22-year-old son of a department store owner. *1933.*

**THE 30s**

Serving the unemployed at a free kitchen run by a Veterans of Foreign Wars
post in San Francisco on 17th Street. *1931*.

**THE 30s**

Aviatrix Amelia Earhart Putnam in Oakland before her final flight. *1937*.

Victims of violence during a waterfront strike. *1934*.

Wreckage of an airliner at Point Reyes. The plane ran out of gasoline and landed safely at sea, but five persons died when it was washed into the rocks. *1938.*
*Barney Peterson*

**THE 30s**

President Franklin D. Roosevelt waving to the crowd, as Secret Service agents keep watch. *1938*.

Charles and Anne Lindbergh at San Francisco Airport. *1936*.

**THE 30s**

Soccer game action. *1937.*
*Ken McLaughlin*

**THE 30s**

Construction of the Golden Gate Bridge, from Fort Point. *1934.*

*Opposite:* Opening day on the Golden Gate Bridge. *1937.*

**THE 30s**

The San Francisco-Oakland auto ferry on the eve of the opening
of the Bay Bridge. *1936*.

# THE
# 40s

**SPEED GRAPHIC**

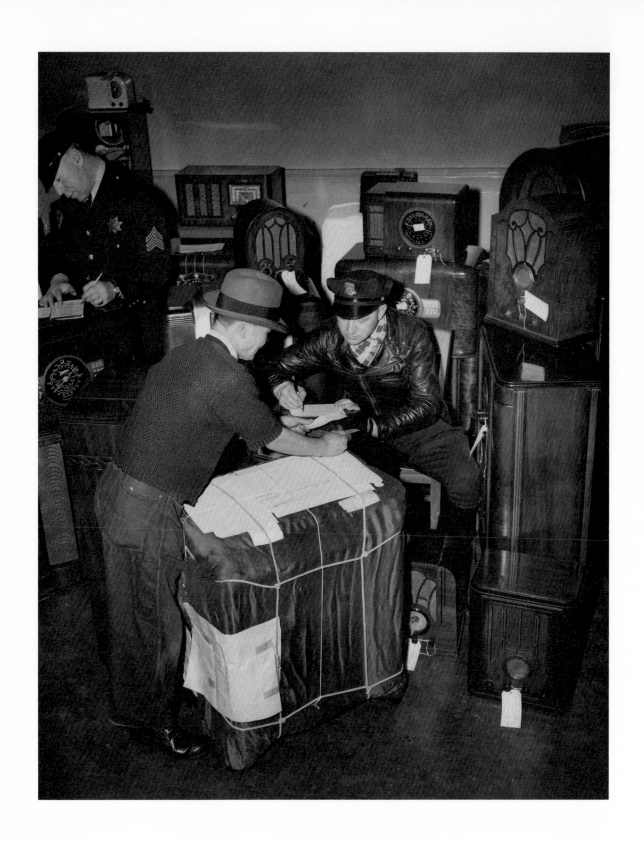

**THE 40s**

A Japanese man turning in his radio to police in San Francisco at the start of World War II. *1941*.

**THE 40s**

*Top:* Reading about D-Day at Commission Markets. *1944.*

A private kissing his girlfriend good-bye before reporting for emergency duty. *1941.*

27

**THE 40s**

Sandbagging the telephone building on Grant Avenue at the start of World War II. *Words were painted on by The Chronicle's art department when the photo first ran. 1941.*

**THE 40s**

The aircraft carrier U.S.S. Boxer passing under the Golden Gate Bridge. *1948.*

**THE 40s**

The fire that razed the California Building during the Golden Gate International Exposition. One fireman died. *1940*.

**THE 40s**

Firemen removing the body of Albert Hudson, one of four firemen killed
in the Hotel Herbert fire. *1946.*
*Aaron Rubino*

**THE 40s**

Donald Panattoni in his Sunset District home confessing to a detective that he killed
his wife, Elaine, and buried her on Mount Tamalpais. *1949*.
*Ken McLaughlin*

**THE 40s**

Eating dinner at San Quentin prison. *1949.*

**THE 40s**

Milton Van Noland during 72 days of flagpole-sitting 50 feet above Van Ness Avenue. *1948.*
*Aaron Rubino*

*Opposite:* One of about 2,000 motorcyclists who terrorized the town of Hollister. *1947.*
*Barney Peterson*

34

**THE 40s**

Questioning an umpire's judgment during a Seals game. *1943.*
*Ken McLaughlin*
The Backyard Farm near the children's playground in Golden Gate Park. *1943.*

Fishing off a pier. *1947.*
*Ken McLaughlin*

**THE 40s**

Sailors, soldiers and civilians celebrating V-J Day on Market Street. *1945*.

# THE
# 50s

**ROLLEIFLEX**

Three crew members died when a United Air Lines Stratocruiser crashed on a test flight. *1951*.
*Bob Campbell*

*Opposite:* The crew escaped when a Pan Am DC-7C crashed at San Francisco's airport. *1959*.
*Bob Campbell*

## THE 50s

A butane gas explosion caused a four-alarm fire that injured 10 persons
at Waverly Place in Chinatown. *1953.*
*Bob Campbell*

**THE 50s**

Roy Buell at the Ferry Building heliport, unaware of the helicopter crashing behind him. *1956*.
*Gordon Peters*

**THE 50s**

A blizzard marooned the passenger train City of San Francisco, with 221 aboard, for four days in the Sierra Nevada. *The Chronicle's photographer and reporter reached the train after skiing two and a half hours. 1952.*
Ken McLaughlin

Witness Evelyn Pancost attacking photographer Jack Gorman at the Cohn divorce trial. *1951.*
*Gordon Peters*

## THE 50s

Flood waters covering downtown Yuba City. A store worker sweeping out water. *1955.*
*Bob Campbell*
*Opposite:* A returning sailor is greeted by his wife. *1952.*
*Gordon Peters*

**THE 50s**

General Douglas MacArthur riding in a parade with San Francisco Mayor Elmer Robinson and California Governor Earl Warren. *1951.*

*Bill Young*

**THE 50s**

President Harry S Truman greeting admirers on an early morning walk
along Van Ness Avenue. *1951.*

*Bill Young*

**THE 50s**

President Dwight D. Eisenhower arriving in San Francisco in his helicopter. *1958.*
*Ken McLaughlin*

Soviet Premier Nikita Khrushchev greeting crowds at the Mark Hopkins Hotel. *1959.*
*Peter Breinig*

Sleeping inmates crowd the San Joaquin county jail holding tank. *1953.*

*Opposite:* A woman looking out from her North Beach pad during the Beatnik era. *1957.*
*Gordon Peters*

## THE 50s

The damaged Hawaiian Pilot limping past Alcatraz after a collision with another freighter. *1953.*
*Gordon Peters*

Sea gulls landing on an ice-covered pond in Golden Gate Park. *1950.*
*Ken McLaughlin*

An irate Sadie Case of Emeryville offering her glasses to the umpire
during a Mother's Day game at Seals Stadium. *1953.*
*Bob Campbell*

**THE 50s**

*Top:* An atomic bomb explosion above Nevada's Yucca Flat creating a false dawn at 4:15 a.m.
*The photograph was taken with a 10-minute exposure. 1953.*
Clem Albers

56

*Bottom, from left:* Inspecting damage after a Bakersfield earthquake. . . *1952.*
*Bob Campbell*
. . .and after a quake in San Francisco. *1957.*
*Duke Downey*

**THE 50s**

Marilyn Monroe and Joe DiMaggio waiting for a judge to marry them at City Hall. *1954*.
*Art Frisch*

# THE
# 60s

**NIKON F**

A cable car accident at Powell and Market streets that injured seven persons. *1966.*
*Art Frisch*
*Opposite:* Battling the $2.5 million St. Mary's Cathedral fire. *1962.*

Police dousing demonstrators and dragging them from the steps inside City Hall,
site of a House Un-American Activities Committee hearing. *1960*.
*Bob Campbell, Peter Breinig*

**THE 60s**

*Top:* The Beatles arriving for their final concert. They played at Candlestick Park. *1966.*
*Bob Campbell*

Policeman tending to a swooning fan before a Beatles concert at the Cow Palace. *1964.*
*Barney Peterson*

Officers checking dancer Yvonne Dangers' street clothes
after a North Beach topless nightclub raid. *1965*.
*Ken McLaughlin*

**THE 60s**

Julia Cooney, a passenger ship waitress, after a firefighting course
at the Navy's school on Treasure Island. *1960.*
*Gordon Peters*

Polk Street beatniks. *1962.*
*Barney Peterson*

Arnold Palmer playing in the U.S. Open at the Olympic Club. He lost. *1966.*
*Bob Campbell*

George Swyers of the Akron-Goodyear Wingfoots leaping over Paul Neuman
of the San Francisco Investors. *1960*.
*Gordon Peters*

**THE 60s**

*Top:* Indian students beginning the 19-month occupation of Alcatraz Island. *1969.*
Federal officials making a sweep of the island after reclaiming it. *1971.*
*Vince Maggiora*

## THE 60s

UC Berkeley students demonstrating against the Vietnam War. *1969.*
*Vince Maggiora*
President Lyndon B. Johnson shaking hands in Union Square during a visit. *1964.*

**THE 60s**

Carrying away an injured man during the Hunters Point riot. *1966.*
*Bob Campbell*

## THE 60s

San Francisco State University President S.I. Hayakawa after pulling
the plug on protesters' microphones. *1968.*
*Gordon Peters*

Presidential candidate Richard Nixon campaigning in Chinatown
with his wife, Pat. *1968.*
*Gordon Peters*

# THE
# 70s

**NIKON F2**

*Left:* Patty Hearst leaving jail for her first court appearance after her capture. *1975.*
Susan Gilbert

*Right:* Released by presidential pardon and sporting a gift from her future husband. *1979.*
Gary Fong

## THE 70s

**Harvey Milk leading the Gay Freedom Parade down Market Street.** *1978.*
*Terry Schmitt*

Dan White being arrested in the slayings of Mayor George Moscone
and Supervisor Harvey Milk. *1978.*
*John Storey*

**THE 70s**

*From top:* Cars burning in the aftermath of rioting at City Hall by gays . . .
*Susan Gilbert*

. . . following the manslaughter conviction of Dan White for the murders of Moscone and Milk. *1979.*
*John Storey*

79

Trick roper Montie Montana lassoing Supervisor Dianne Feinstein
in ceremonies before the Grand Nationals. *1970.*
*Joe Rosenthal*

## THE 70s

Judge Charles Goff knocked down by pickets during a city employees' strike. *1976.*
*Art Frisch*
An elated supporter hugging George Moscone after he was elected mayor. *1975.*

**THE 70s**

A child in the first planeload of Vietnamese orphans flown out during the fall
of Saigon to Oakland International Airport. *1975.*
*Jerry Telfer*

A Coast Guard helicopter rescuing a climber who fell near the Cliff House. *1975.*
*Art Frisch*

**THE 70s**

Protesting ROTC during a Columbus Day parade. *1971.*
*Greg Peterson*

**THE 70s**

*Top:* Policeman thwarting an attempt to tear down the International Hotel. *1977.*
John O'Hara

A murder victim in the Minna Street alley. *1972.*
Vince Maggiora

A prisoner on San Quentin's death row when the Supreme Court upheld the death penalty. *1976.*
*Susan Gilbert*
A waiter accidentally setting himself on fire during a Fol de Rol party. *1971.*

A policeman framed in the speak hole at the desk where a sergeant
was shot to death at Ingleside station. *1971.*
*Ken McLaughlin*

**THE 70s**

The first suicide under a BART train, at Berkeley station. *1974.*
*Stephanie Maze*

West Oakland residents attempting to chase prostitutes
from their neighborhood. *1979.*
*Vici MacDonald*

Celebrants arriving at the Hilton Hotel for a Hookers' Ball. *1976.*
*Stephanie Maze*

**THE 70s**

Dizzy Gillespie giving a free jazz lesson
at Raphael Weill Elementary School in San Francisco. *1976.*
*Susan Gilbert*

## THE 70s

*Left:* The Goodyear blimp passing by the nearly completed Transamerica pyramid. *1973.*
*Art Frisch*

*Top:* A San Francisco Zoo elephant reaching for a snack. *1975.*
*Clem Albers*

**THE 70s**

*Bottom left:* A deer on Angel Island hoping for handouts from park rangers. *1976.*
*Gary Fong*

*Bottom right:* Fun at the carousel in Golden Gate Park. *1975.*
*Gary Fong*

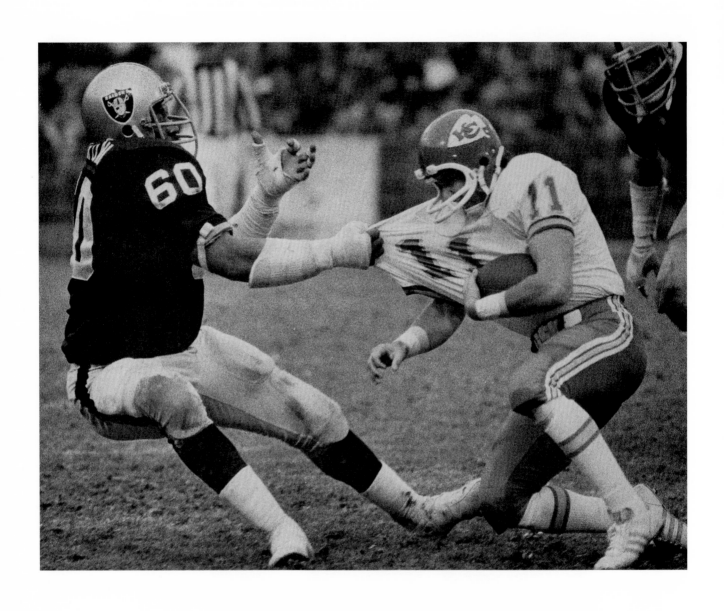

## THE 70s

Otis Sistrunk of the Oakland Raiders dragging down
Kansas City Chiefs' quarterback Tony Adams. *1975.*
*Jerry Telfer*

The Warriors' Butch Beard jumping in the championship game against the Bullets. *1975*.
*Stephanie Maze*

John Montefusco hugging Gary Lavelle after the Giants won the season opener. *1976*.
*Gary Fong*

**THE 70s**

*Top:* President Gerald Ford ducking Sara Jane Moore's assassination attempt. *1975.*
*Gary Fong*

The media interviewing a demonstrator barricaded inside the Nicaraguan consulate. *1978.*
*Jerry Telfer*

**THE 70s**

The pilot filming Jimmy Carter as he leaves his campaign plane. *1976.*
*Susan Gilbert*

**THE 70s**

Snow covering the hills of Marin County. *1976.*
*Art Frisch*

# THE
# 80s

**NIKON F3**

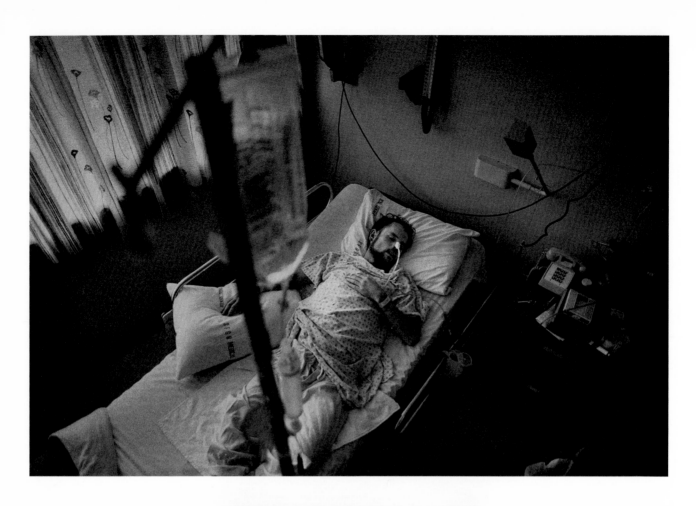

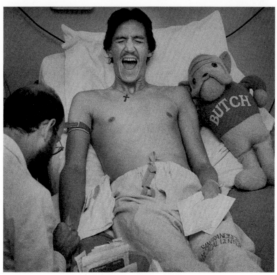

**THE 80s**

*Top:* Deotis McMather, dying of AIDS at San Francisco General Hospital. *1983.*
Bruce Schneider undergoing treatment in San Francisco General's AIDS ward. *1983.*
*Steve Ringman*

*Top*: Gary Walsh talking about life with AIDS. *1983.*
The gay community marching in support of more federal funds for AIDS research. *1983.*
*Steve Ringman*

The elite Navy flying team, the Blue Angels, crossing Highway 101
on the way to Moffett Field. *1983*.
*Gary Fong*

Tugboats attempting to free the U.S.S. Enterprise after it ran
aground on a sand bar near Alameda. *1983.*
*Art Frisch*

Police raiding a suspected drug dealer's house
in the Mission District. *1981.*
*Frederic Larson*

**THE 80s**

*Top:* Police clearing a path for a sheriff's bus during a UC Berkeley anti-nuclear protest. *1984.*
*Gary Fong*

A policeman extricating a prisoner from cell bars; he said he was just reaching for cigarets. *1980.*
*Frederic Larson*

**THE 80s**

A fireman rescuing a toddler from a five-alarm fire in the Tenderloin. *1983.*
*Frederic Larson*

*Top:* Rescuing a woman from a fire at the Cathedral Hill Hotel. Two persons died. *1983.*
Steve Ringman
Residents of a burning Richmond apartment building calling to firemen for help. *1985.*
Gary Fong

Mayor Dianne Feinstein christening the rebuilt cable car system. *1984*.
*Chris Stewart*

*Opposite:* Living on the streets in San Francisco. *1986*.
*Steve Ringman*

Newly named presidential and vice presidential candidates at the Democratic convention. *1984*.
*Brant Ward*

George Bush joking with the press while campaigning in Chinatown. *1985*.
*Jerry Telfer*

President Ronald Reagan reacting to a joke told by Queen Elizabeth during her speech
at the De Young Museum. *1983.*
*Steve Ringman*

**THE 80s**

Former President Richard Nixon addressing newspaper executives in San Francisco. *1986.*
*Brant Ward*

Vice presidential candidate Geraldine Ferraro campaigning with the help of Willie Brown. *1984.*
*Brant Ward*

A young visitor to Steinhart Aquarium trying to make contact with a dolphin. *1986*.
*Tom Levy*

Humphrey, the humpback whale, making his way back to the Pacific Ocean
after spending a month in the Delta. *1985*.
*Brant Ward*

Getting too close to a 15-foot great white shark at Bill's Ranch Market in Pittsburg. *1985.*
*Chris Stewart*

A picture of winery owner Stephen Zellerbach. *1986.*
*John O'Hara*

**THE 80s**

A groom's attention wandering as he and his bride await their civil ceremony at City Hall. *1985.*
*Tom Levy*

**THE 80s**

*Top:* A South of Market bartender taking a break. *1986.*
*Liz Hafalia*

Patas monkeys that escaped from the zoo in their cage after being recaptured. *1985.*
*Vince Maggiora*

117

Anna Hauptmann, whose husband, Richard, was executed in the Lindbergh baby kidnaping.
*Chris Stewart*

*Opposite:* A historical trolley car delivered by the Soviet Union to the Muni car barn. *1986.*
*Tom Levy*

**THE 80s**

*Top:* Checking out one of the Chippendale male strippers at the Circle Star Theater. *1986.*
*John O'Hara*

A prosthetic eyeball. *1986.*
*John O'Hara*

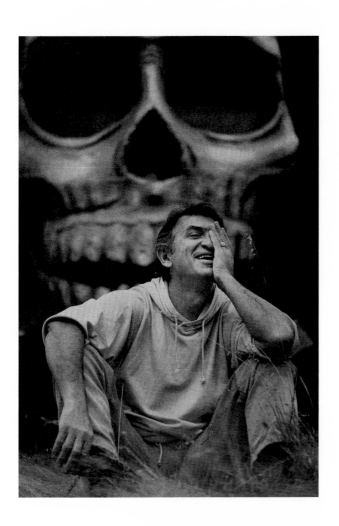

*Left:* Rock impresario Bill Graham relaxing at his Mill Valley home. *1985.*
*Steve Ringman*

*Right:* Rock star Peter Gabriel playing off the stage lighting during a concert in Oakland. *1986.*
*Deanne Fitzmaurice*

**THE 80s**

Mikhail Baryshnikov and Alessandra Ferri of American Ballet Theatre rehearsing. *1986.*
*Tom Levy*

Two San Franciscans protesting toxic chemicals in the city's sewer system. *1985.*
*Chris Stewart*

Recording the moment before the Gay Freedom Day parade. *1985*.
*Steve Ringman*

**THE 80s**

An anti-apartheid demonstrator being arrested by UC Berkeley police. *1986*.
*Mike Maloney*

A cat that survived the Lexington reservoir fire. *1985*.
*Eric Luse*

**THE 80s**

*Top:* A bomb exploding at Harvey's Casino in Stateline, Nevada. *1980.*
*Frederic Larson*

A girl returning to school in Cokeville, Wyo., where she and classmates were held hostage. *1986.*
*Chris Stewart*

Oanh Kim Tieu, 15, grieving at the funeral of her parents,
who were found slain in their San Francisco home. *1984.*
*Eric Luse*

A farewell to the crew of the Jack Jr., who died when their fishing boat
was rammed by a tanker. *1986.*
*Vince Maggiora*

## THE 80s

*Left:* A man jumping to his death after losing his job and his lover. *1980.*
Eric Luse

*Right:* A mother mourning her son, killed by police when he aimed a toy gun at them. *1986.*
Bryan Moss

A plane, shot down in the civil war, lying on the hillside
above a Nicaraguan cemetery. *1986.*
*Steve Ringman*

**THE 80s**

*Above:* Doctors in an emergency triage after a hospital collapsed in the
Mexico City earthquake. *Opposite, top:* Soldiers guarding a makeshift morgue. *Bottom:* Residents
grieving as victims are pulled from rubble. *1985.*
*Eric Luse, Chris Stewart*

**THE 80s**

*Top:* Navy personnel fighting the wind at the All-Star festivities in Candlestick Park. *1984.*
*Brant Ward*
A fan sunning herself during an Oakland A's game. *1982.*
*Gary Fong*

Giants outfielders Robbie Thompson and Jose Arribe going for the ball during a game against the Dodgers. *1986.*

*Frederic Larson*

**THE 80s**

*Top:* Willie Mays covering his ears from the din after being introduced on opening day. *1986.*
*Mike Maloney*

San Ramon High School football player Tim Morony on the bench with a hand injury. *1986.*
*Deanne Fitzmaurice*

Cal coach Joe Kapp being carried off the field after his last game, an upset defeat of Stanford in the Big Game. *1986.*
*Frederic Larson*

Heavyweight boxer Larry Holmes displaying his championship belt for the press
at his weigh-in before fighting Muhammad Ali in Las Vegas. *1980.*
*Frederic Larson*

**THE 80s**

Joe Montana and Dwight Clark leaving the field after making a 49er touchdown. *1985.*
*Frederic Larson*

**THE 80s**

*Top:* A pointer in training flushes out a quail near Dixon. *1985.*
*Brant Ward*
Yellow labrador retriever waiting for master Chuck Harrison to bag a Christmas goose. *1985.*
*Eric Luse*

**THE 80s**

*Top:* Waves battering a sea wall at Stinson Beach. *1983.*
*Peter Breinig*

San Jose residents surveying the damage to their home caused by a flood. *1983.*
*Gary Fong*

Lightning over San Francisco Bay, as seen from Vista Point. *1984.*
*Gary Fong*

Mount St. Helens spewing ash. *1980.*
*John Storey*

St. Ignatius Church in the Richmond District poking through the fog. *1986.*
*Frederic Larson*

Schoolgirls braving the elements. *1983.*
*Steve Ringman*

# CREDITS